A TEST PREPARATION
and SEMINAR GUIDE *for*

EFFECTIVE
Police
Leadership

Moving Beyond
Management

Compatible with Both 1st and 2nd Edition Books

A Study Guide Dedicated to
Police Officers in Their Pursuits of
Excellence and Successful Achievement
on Promotional Exams

THOMAS E. BAKER

Looseleaf
Law Publications, Inc.

43-08 162nd Street
Flushing, NY 11358
www.LooseleafLaw.com
800-647-5547

This publication is intended for use with
EFFECTIVE POLICE LEADERSHIP
Moving Beyond Management
1st and 2nd Editions
by
Thomas E. Baker
ISBN 1-932777-27-X – 298 Pages – Softcover
To order a copy of this book, additional copies of this test guide or a free catalog, contact us.
Toll-free (800) 647-5547
Fax (718) 539-0941
www.LooseleafLaw.com

TABLE OF CONTENTS

INTRODUCTION

The opportunity to grow professionally and maximize one's leadership potential is a lifetime process. The most successful candidates imagine the possibilities, prepare and follow through professionally. One does not simply study for the promotional exam; the focus is on lifetime leadership responsibilities. Therefore, careers require continuous strategic preparation for selfless service.

In the twenty-first century, the emphasis will be on police competence and character, not length of service. Scholarship and training play a significant role in the competitive selection opportunities for few leadership positions. Therefore, successful leaders always prepare for the responsibility of the next highest rank. Arriving does mean merely passing the test, being prepared for the role is more important.

EFFECTIVE POLICE LEADERSHIP: *Moving Beyond Management* is designed for police officers. However, the book does have cross over potential for colleges/universities as a textbook. The book and study guide encourages a flexible format to meet the needs of police officers, police instructors and professors. Moreover, the book is an inspirational reader for police officers who seek command and leadership responsibilities.

EFFECTIVE POLICE LEADERSHIP: *Moving Beyond Management* is an educational experience and learning modality that has training potential. It deliberately focuses on reader friendly syntax and fonts rather than dissertation writing. The sentences are active rather than passive and the paragraphs are condensed.

The underlying foundation for the book is the systematic instructional design. Excellence in education and training requires a roadmap for learners. The roadmap should include a philosophy, goals, objectives and evaluation process. For an example, refer to **Figure 1: A Systematic Design for Instruction.**

Figure 1: Systematic Design for Instruction & Learning

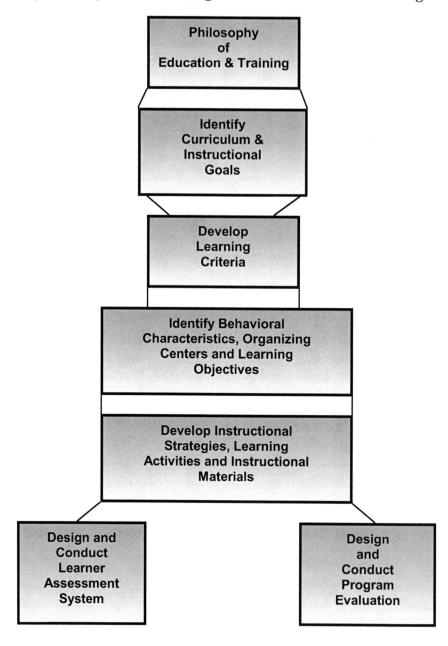

Tips for Police Oral Board Conduct

Report to the board on time, salute, stand at attention and wait for directions. Be seated only by request from one of the board members.

- ❖ The candidate should communicate strengths and experience relevant to the Police Department.
- ❖ Candidates should be diplomatic and tactful, not evasive.
- ❖ Maintain excellent eye-to-eye contact.
- ❖ Answer the questions honestly.
- ❖ The answer is not as important as your ability to communicate to the board members.
- ❖ Smile and keep your sense of humor without sacrificing your dignity.
- ❖ Present a balanced point of view, recognizing multiple slides to any argument.
- ❖ Answer the question but do not over answer and elaborate too much.
- ❖ Maintain your composure and do not lose control or be provoked by any statements or questions posed by a board member, including "hot topics."
- ❖ The questions about your contribution to the police department fall into three categories: (1) Why are you interested in serving in a higher level of responsibility? (2) How would you contribute in this new capacity? (3) How would your leadership improve the morale of police officers and department?
- ❖ The second category of questions fall into hypothetical situations: (1) What would you do in this kind of situation? (2) How would you coordinate with others? (3) How would your leadership make a difference?
- ❖ The third category of questions fall into stress questions: (1) These questions elicit a stress response in the candidate, (2) The questions are offered as interruption to a former questions to off-balance the candidate, and (3) The topic may even be personal, and designed to see how you react. An example might be: Have you ever been frightened and how did you handle the fear?

- ❖ Do not lose control if a board member attempts to "push your buttons." They may be trying to see how you handle yourself when confronted.
- ❖ Do not make it a personal contest of wills between you and the Board.
- ❖ It is not what you say, but how you say it!
- ❖ Thank the Board at the end of the oral interview.

SAMPLE ORAL BOARD QUESTIONS:

1. Describe your career vision, goals and objectives.
2. Why are you qualified for this promotion?
3. Describe an ideal job description for the rank you are attempting to achieve.
4. If promoted, what can you do for the Department to improve policing?
5. What can you do to improve the Police Department?
6. How will your leadership philosophy contribute to the welfare of the men and women of the Police Department?
7. What is your philosophy of policing?
8. How would you increase morale in your area of authority?
9. **Hypothetical Question:** You are experiencing difficulty with an older officer who arrives late for work. He has the smell of alcohol on his breath and behaves in a belligerent and insubordinate manner. How would you handle this situation?
10. **Hypothetical Question:** You have information that one of your sergeants is dating a subordinate on his shift. This is creating a morale problem for officers. She is in his direct command authority and answers to him daily on the shift. How would you handle this situation?
11. **Hypothetical Situation:** A mob has gathered outside of city hall and is threatening the mayor and city council. One member of the crowd is an active police officer. What key factors would you consider to correct the problem?
12. **Hypothetical Situation:** You discover that your officers have little training in community oriented and problem oriented policing. There is considerable friction in the minority community, conflict and violence is possible. What would you do to improve the training and social climate?

13. What are the **three most important** issues facing the Police Department?
14. What are the **most difficult issues** facing the Police Department?
15. Which issue would you address first?

MULTIPLE CHOICE QUESTIONS

Multiple-choice questions come in three basic formats. Most of the questions require recognition. Examine question "A" for example:

Format 1

Question A: The four stages of group development include all of the following except:

A. Forming
B. Storming
C. Norming
D. Trust **("D" choice is correct)**

Format 2

The more difficult format of multiple-choice questions requires reasoning and presents a concept for indirect measurement. Examine question "B" for an example:

Question B: When the result of a leadership attempt is that the person does what the leader wanted, that is _____ leadership.

A. Effective
B. Successful **("B" choice is correct)**
C. Both successful and effective
D. Insufficient information to determine.

The third type of multiple-choice question is a hypothetical situation that requires your reasoning skills. Examine Question "C" for an example of this type of multiple-choice question.

Question C: In the past, your department has encountered problems with riots at the local football stadium. As part of your department's response plan, you have predetermined a site for a command post. Which of the following recommendations would be most appropriate?

A. A fire station near the scene of potential riots
B. An abandoned high school **("B" choice is correct) The fire station would present command conflicts and is too close to the riot area. Rioters may overwhelm the temporary command post.**
C. Both of the above
D. None of the above

EXAMINATION SCORING

In most cases one should guess if one does not know the answer if each question is scored against all of the questions. However, some tests are scored on the percentage of correct answers and the candidate may be penalized for guessing. How the test is scored is an important consideration. Ask the proctor how the answers how will be scored before the examination starts.

Chapter Objectives
and
Practice Examination
Questions

CHAPTER 1

PHILOSOPHY: COMMUNITY-ORIENTED POLICING

LEARNING OBJECTIVES

1. Discuss the term "community-oriented policing."
2. Identify community-oriented policing values.
3. Describe how to implement community-oriented policing.
4. Describe some community-oriented policing problems.
5. Define traditional policing.
6. Identify some role conflicts that police officers may encounter with the community-oriented policing philosophy.
7. Describe some of the elements of problem-oriented policing.
8. List elements of the SARA Planning Process.
9. Describe some of the basic leadership elements of a Neighborhood Watch Program.

QUESTIONS

1. As lieutenant and commander of the Community Policing Unit, you understand that the strategic arm of community policing remains:

   A. POSDCORB
   B. SARA
   C. LEAA
   D. None of the above

2. In addition, as the Commander, your subordinates will apply the SARA model that includes all of the following except:

   A. Scanning
   B. Analysis
   C. Selective enforcement
   D. Response
   E. Assessment

3. **Community Neighborhood Watch Programs include five basic steps. The first step is:**

   A. Train the officers
   B. Plan strategies
   C. Develop meaningful projects
   D. POSDCORB
   E. None of the above

4. **A community Neighborhood Watch Program includes five basic steps. The second step is:**

   A. Train the officers
   B. Develop meaningful projects
   C. Assess community needs
   D. None of the above

5. **A community Neighborhood Watch Program includes five basic steps. The fifth step is:**

   A. Train the officers
   B. Assess community needs
   C. Select and train volunteers
   D. Develop meaningful projects

Chapter 2
POLICE LEADERSHIP AND PROFESSIONAL ETHICS

LEARNING OBJECTIVES

1. List some of the elements of the Police Code of Ethics.
2. Describe attributes of an ethical climate.
3. Recite the Law Enforcement Oath of Honor.
4. List the characteristics of ethical police behavior.
5. Conduct a personal assessment of professional and ethical standards.
6. Describe how to build an ethical climate.
7. List the key characteristics of an unethical and ethical climate.
8. Describe the professional ethics model.
9. List four requirements for ethical decision-making.
10. Describe some of the rationalizations that can lead to misconduct on the part of police leaders.

QUESTIONS

1. **In the EFFECTIVE POLICE LEADERSHIP case study, Major Drone achieved his rank because of his _____.**

   A. Expert power
   B. Tactical expertise
   C. Self-serving behavior
   D. Effectiveness

2. **In the EFFECTIVE POLICE LEADERSHIP case study, MAJ Drone lives by the leadership style that includes:**

   A. Reward and coercive power
   B. Power hungry
   C. Self-interest
   D. All of the above

3. **The basic Police Code of Ethics was adopted by:**

    A. California Peace Officers' Association
    B. International Association of Chiefs of Police
    C. National Sheriff's Association
    D. The Federal Bureau of Investigation

4. **What level of leader is responsible for creating the appropriate ethical climate?**

    A. Sergeants
    B. Middle managers/leaders
    C. Chief and senior leaders
    D. None of the above

5. **Self-assessment requires understanding one's:**

    A. Personality
    B. Values
    C. Strengths
    D. Weaknesses
    E. All of the above

CHAPTER 3
POLICE SENIOR LEADERSHIP

LEARNING OBJECTIVES

1. Discuss the role of the Chief of Police as a strategic leader.
2. Define senior leadership.
3. Identify essential senior leadership responsibilities.
4. Define how senior leaders use indirect leadership to implement their basic leadership functions.
5. Define vision.
6. Describe how to implement vision.
7. Describe the four senior leadership functions.
8. Describe three senior leadership imperatives.
9. Describe the basic elements of social power.

QUESTIONS

1. **In the EFFECTIVE POLICE LEADERSHIP case study, Chief Shane Piland emphasized:**

   A. Directing traffic
   B. Crime control
   C. Vision
   D. None of the above

2. **Power is defined as:**

   A. A disgusting subject
   B. Influence potential
   C. The absolute ability to get A to do something A doesn't want to do.
   D. The absolute ability to resist doing something that A wants you to do.

3. **Legitimate power is:**

   A. The power of someone who knows.
   B. The power from being liked.
   C. The power associated with the position held by the leader.
   D. The power of knowing the "right" persons.

4. **Referent power is:**

A. The power of being liked and admired by others because of personality.
B. The power of knowing to whom to refer difficult questions.
C. The power of knowing where to look up answers to difficult questions.
D. The power of knowing the answers to difficult questions.

5. **The power base most strongly associated with follower satisfaction tend to be:**

A. Coercive and reward
B. Reward and legitimate
C. Expert and referent
D. No clear evidence

6. **Coercive power is most effective at achieving compliance from:**

A. Followers at a low level of readiness.
B. Followers at a moderate level of readiness.
C. Followers at a high level of readiness.
D. None of the above.

7. **Expert power is most effective at influencing:**

A. Followers of low readiness level.
B. Followers of moderate readiness level.
C. Followers of high readiness level.
D. None of the above.

8. **Senior leaders enhance ethical behaviors when they focus on:**

A. Junior leaders
B. Middle Managers
C. Administration and policy
D. None of the above

9. **Senior leaders lead primarily through:**

A. Direct leadership
B. Indirect leadership
C. First-line supervisors
D. None of the above

10. **Senior leaders can develop and sustain a positive ethical climate by all of the following except:**

A. Developing trust
B. Listening
C. Tolerating all mistakes
D. None of the above

10

NOTES

CHAPTER 4
MIDDLE MANAGEMENT
AND LEADERSHIP

LEARNING OBJECTIVES

1. Describe the self-assessment process.
2. Define the term "middle manager."
3. Define the term "management."
4. Identify the POSDCORB management functions.
5. Differentiate between management and leadership.
6. Describe the role of the manager.
7. List the characteristics of McGregor's Theory X and Theory Y.
8. Differentiate between the following terms: coaching, building teams and empowering.
9. List four management functions.
10. Describe Theory Z.
11. Describe Quality-Circle Programs.

QUESTIONS

1. **Management and leadership are different in that:**

   A. Management is a broader term than leadership.
   B. Management is a specialized form of leadership.
   C. Leadership is an ethical concept; management is a practical one.
   D. There is no difference.

2. **The quality leadership stresses:**

   A. Theory "X"
   B. Theory "Y"
   C. Theory "Z"
   D. None of the above

3. **Quality circle teams emphasize:**

    A. Theory "Y"
    B. Theory "X"
    C. Theory "Z"
    D. None of the above

4. **When Captain Gordon Alexander replaced Captain Josh Williams, in EFFECTIVE POLICE LEADERSHIP, what did he do that changed the organizational climate?**

    A. Reduced the level of formal power
    B. Changed outdated regulations
    C. None of the above
    D. Both of the above

5. **Theory X was developed by:**

    A. Baker
    B. Drucker
    C. Hersey
    D. Bradford
    E. McGregor

6. **The first "O" in POSDCORB stands for:**

    A. Orders
    B. Objectives
    C. Organizing
    D. Observation
    E. Obedience

7. **The backbone of the department, and responsible for the attainment of all police objectives, is the:**

    A. Chief
    B. Patrol division
    C. Detective division
    D. Community-relations officer and section

8. As police lieutenant/captain, you acknowledge that mentoring and coaching requires:

    A. Explanation of purpose
    B. Show how it is done
    C. Provide feedback
    D. Expresses confidence
    E. All of the above

9. The Chief has requested that the captains/lieutenants establish a management by objective program. In a management by objectives (MBO) program:

    1. The manager sets objectives for followers
    2. Followers set objectives for themselves
    3. Each member is provided with organizational objectives
    4. Manager and follower agree on the follower's performance goals

NOTES

CHAPTER 5
SERGEANTS AND POLICE OFFICERS

LEARNING OBJECTIVES

1. Define leadership.
2. Identify essential sergeant leadership responsibilities.
3. Define the leadership framework.
4. Distinguish between directive and supportive behaviors.
5. Define the four basic leadership styles.
6. Describe the various developmental levels.
7. Apply the appropriate leadership style to the follower's developmental level.
8. Assess the role of the police sergeant in sustaining the ethical climate.
9. Discuss the elements of transforming leadership.

QUESTIONS

1. **The emphasis in Situational Leadership is on:**

   A. The situational variables
   B. The behavior of the leader in relation to the follower(s)
   C. Task behavior
   D. Relationship behavior

2. **Task behavior is:**

   A. Spelling out the duties and responsibilities of the individual or group
   B. Telling people what to do
   C. Telling people how, when, where, and who's to do something
   D. All of the above

3. **Relationship behavior is:**

   A. Engaging in two-way or multi-way communication
   B. Touching people, and telling them how you feel
   C. Encouraging followers to be open about their personal lives with you
   D. All of the above

4. **If a leader's style uses high amounts of task behavior, the leader will use _____ amounts of relationship behavior.**

   A. Low
   B. High
   C. Sometimes low, sometimes high
   D. Impossible to tell, the two are independent of one another

5. **A new project comes across your desk, and one of your personnel should be assigned to do it. Generally, projects are assigned in rotation, and it is Sgt Fred's turn to get a project. Sgt. Fred is usually five to ten minutes late to work. Do you think Fred can handle this project?**

   A. You will not give Fred the project; he is unwilling since he cannot even get to work on time.
   B. You will not give Sgt. Fred the project hoping that he will get the idea that he should be on time to work.
   C. Fred's tardiness may not affect your decision at all. You cannot tell by looking at his tardiness record.
   D. None of the above.

6. **If Sgt. Fred is willing to do the tasks involved in the project, does that ensure he will complete it competently?**

   A. Yes
   B. Probably, willingness is the most important
   C. No, he must also be able.
   D. No, a person who is always late is just not a willing worker.

7. If the appropriate leadership style to use with Sgt. Fred regarding getting to work on time is S1, what does that mean?

   A. Leaving him alone
   B. Facilitating his discovery of his own solutions for the problem
   C. Telling him that you do not value him as an employee
   D. Stating to him directly that the workday begins at 8:00 a.m.

8. If the project involves tasks that Sgt. Fred enjoys and is good at doing, the proper leadership style to use with him on that project is probably:

   A. S1, telling
   B. S2, selling
   C. S3, participating
   D. S4, delegating

9. Sgt. Grace Jones another employee in your department, has just been assigned a project. She has been in the department for only five weeks, but has proven to be a real go-getter. She asks many questions, and she reads all the material regarding department operations. The appropriate leadership style for Grace in this, her first project, is probably:

   A. S1, Telling
   B. S2, Selling
   C. S3, Participating
   D. S4, Delegating

10. In the above example, Sgt. Grace Jones' readiness level is:

   A. R1, Unable and unwilling or insecure
   B. R2, Unable but willing or confident
   C. R3, Able but unwilling or insecure
   D. R4, Able and willing or confident

11. The style which incorporates below average amounts of task behavior and above average amounts of relationship behavior is:

A. S1, Telling
B. S2, Selling
C. S3, Participating
D. S4, Delegating

12. If the appropriate leadership style for a given situation is S1, but the leader can't use that style, what is the next most probably successful style?

A. S2, Selling
B. S3, Participating
C. S4, Delegating
D. There is no next most probably successful style. If the appropriate style is S1, that is what the leader should use.

13. How should Situational Leadership be used?

A. As a developmental tool
B. As a way to determine the one best way to treat each individual
C. As a way to help individuals and groups increase their readiness
D. Both A and C

14. Once the leader has assessed the readiness of an individual or group, can the leader go ahead and determine appropriate leadership style?

A. No, first the leader must assess what aspects of activities to influence
B. No, first the leader must assess the willingness of the individual or group
C. No, first the leader must assess the skill level of the individual or group
D. Yes

15. **Part of Sgt. Fred's job is doing the quarterly budget reports. He is very good at these, and never has to be reminded of them. Fred's readiness level is:**

    A. R4
    B. R3
    C. R4 for the budget reports, unable to determine for the rest of his job
    D. Insufficient information to determine

16. **Components of readiness include:**

    A. Achievement motivation, ability to set high but realistic goals
    B. Education
    C. Experience
    D. All of the above

17. **A major difference between ability and willingness is:**

    A. Ability does not fluctuate widely, while willingness may.
    B. Willingness does not fluctuate widely while ability may.
    C. Ability may be lost from not using it, but not willingness.
    D. There is no major difference between willingness and ability

18. **The police sergeant in the field of law enforcement:**

    A. Is a noncommissioned officer
    B. Is a commissioned officer
    C. Has the same status as a corporal
    D. None of the above

19. **According to the research, sergeants spend approximately _____ % of their time in face-to-face contact with their officers. The best choice is:**

    A. 50%
    B. 40%
    C. 30%
    D. 10%

20. The components of the leadership skill mix:

    A. human relations, conceptual, and psychological
    B. empathy, honesty and trust
    C. human relations, theoretical, and psychological
    D. human relations, conceptual, and technical
    E. human relations, technical, and practical

CHAPTER 6
MOTIVATION AND POLICE PERSONNEL

LEARNING OBJECTIVES

1. Define "motivation."
2. Describe the role of senior leaders, middle managers and first line supervisors involving the motivation of police officers.
3. Discuss goal-oriented behavior in the police department.
4. Define the elements of an objective.
5. Describe a work plan.
6. List methods that may be used to help reverse police cynicism.
7. List the steps in an effective disciplinary process.

QUESTIONS

1. **Discipline should be considered when:**

    A. The leader feels the followers need to be kept on their toes.
    B. Followers begin to behave at lower readiness than in the past.
    C. The leader's boss indicates that followers have a performance problem.
    D. The leader is tired of the performance.

2. **Which of the following is not a key to a reprimand?**

    A. Specific
    B. As soon as possible
    C. Reaffirm
    D. Intellectualize

3. **_____ is clearly an activator.**

    A. Motivation
    B. Behavior modification
    C. Goal setting
    D. Performance appraisal

4. Participatory management is:

    A. Always most effective
    B. Most effective in the U.S. and other similar nations
    C. Very ineffective in areas of low task relevant readiness
    D. Both B and C

5. According to EFFECTIVE POLICE LEADERSHIP, Sergeant Paul Trevino's major leadership task was_____.

    A. Define the mission
    B. Describe his personal goals
    C. Write the task assignment
    D. Develop his relationship with the informal leader

CHAPTER 7
POLICE TRAINING

LEARNING OBJECTIVES

1. Describe the essential outcomes of training.
2. Define strategic training.
3. Identify consequences of inadequate police training.
4. Describe the relationship between training and motivation.
5. Compare senior, middle manager and first line supervisor training responsibilities.
6. Discuss the legal liabilities that may be the consequence of inadequate police training.
7. Identify the steps involved in the development of strategic planning and training.
8. Define active learning.

QUESTIONS

1. **In the EFFECTIVE POLICE LEADERSHIP case study: Captain Shannon Brooks emphasized:**

    A. Conflict
    B. Training
    C. COPPS
    D. SARA

2. **According to EFFECTIVE POLICE LEADERSHIP, strategic training includes:**

    A. Community-oriented policing training
    B. Police ethics training
    C. Use of force training
    D. Civil liabilities
    E. All of the above

3. According to EFFECTIVE POLICE LEADERSHIP, who are the police training managers?

   A. Sergeants
   B. Chief and senior leaders
   C. Middle managers/leaders
   D. All of the above

4. According to EFFECTIVE POLICE LEADERSHIP, who are the primary trainers?

   A. Sergeants
   B. Chief and senior leaders
   C. Middle managers/leaders
   D. All of the above

5. According to EFFECTIVE POLICE LEADERSHIP, the most effective training is:

   A. Lecture oriented
   B. Visually oriented
   C. Performance oriented
   D. None of the above

CHAPTER 8
HUMAN RESOURCES MANAGEMENT

LEARNING OBJECTIVES

1. Identify the various strategic objectives necessary for achieving the potential of human resources management.
2. Describe the need for quality police personnel.
3. Identify some of the key federal legislation that ensures the civil rights of an applicant.
4. Define vicarious liability.
5. Define the Management by Objective System.
6. List the basic advantages and disadvantages of an evaluation system.
7. Discuss some of the limitations concerning promotion and advancement in the Twenty-First Century.
8. List the benefits of a police wellness program.
9. Discuss the steps involved in a police suicide prevention program.

QUESTIONS

1. **According to EFFECTIVE POLICE LEADERSHIP, resource management is:**

   A. Secondary leadership responsibility
   B. Tertiary leadership responsibility
   C. Core leadership responsibility
   D. None of the above

2. **As the personnel unit commander, one of your applicants has filed a racial discrimination grievance under _____ which prohibits racial discrimination concerning employment, hiring and placement.**

   A. Title IX
   B. ADIA Act
   C. The Civil Rights Act
   D. None of the above

3. You are serving as a shift commander. One of your sergeants asks for clarification on the rating scale. You explain that police personnel evaluations are based on:

    A. Effort
    B. Ability
    C. Direction
    D All of the above

4. The sergeant complains about the time involved in the paperwork and feels that police personnel evaluations are a waste of time. As the shift commander, you explain the best personnel evaluations emphasize:

    A. Informality
    B. Formality
    C. Peer evaluations
    D. None of the above

5. As the lieutenant, you further recommend, that for the organizational goals to prevail, Parkinson's "law" suggests that:

    A. Personal goals come before organizational goals
    B. Personal goals equal organizational goals
    C. Organizational goals come before personal goals
    D. Personal goals have nothing to do with organizational goals

CHAPTER 9
CONFLICT MANAGEMENT

LEARNING OBJECTIVES

1. Define conflict.
2. Describe the five stages of conflict.
3. Identify and discuss the most common causes of conflict in police organizations.
4. Describe the differences between functional conflict and dysfunctional conflict.
5. Define intrapersonal and interpersonal conflict.
6. Describe some techniques of conflict management.
7. Discuss some of the strategies for solving interpersonal conflict.
8. Describe how police managers can deal with problem officers.
9. Describe active or focused listening.

QUESTIONS

1. According to the case study in EFFECTIVE POLICE LEADERSHIP, Officer Susan Lightfoot concerned:

A. Positive praise
B. Letter of commendation
C. Police discipline
D. None of the above

2. According to the case study in EFFECTIVE POLICE LEADERSHIP, Officer Jeb Stone concerned:

A. Positive praise
B. Letter of commendation
C. Police discipline
D. Intrapersonal conflict

3. According to EFFECTIVE POLICE LEADERSHIP, conflict is defined as:

A. Negative
B. Positive
C. Both of the above
D. None of the above

4. According to EFFECTIVE POLICE LEADERSHIP, the first stage of conflict is:

A. Perceived conflict
B. Latent conflict
C. Felt conflict
D. Manifest conflict

5. According to EFFECTIVE POLICE LEADERSHIP, intrapersonal conflict most likely occurs because of:

A. Poor personal relationships
B. Poor training and knowledge
C. Minority relations
D. None of the above

6. According to EFFECTIVE POLICE LEADERSHIP, interpersonal conflict most likely occurs because of:

A. Poor training and knowledge
B. Competitive personalities
C. Organizational problems
D. None of the above

7. According to EFFECTIVE POLICE LEADERSHIP, structural conflict is best described as:

A. Interpersonal conflict
B. Intrapersonal conflict
C. Organizational and structural conflict
D. None of the above

8. According to EFFECTIVE POLICE LEADERSHIP, strategic conflict is best described as:

    A. Informal
    B. Planned intentional
    C. Intrapersonal
    D. None of the above

9. According to EFFECTIVE POLICE LEADERSHIP, the win/win conflict resolution approach is based on:

    A. Conflict is here to stay
    B. Conflict is unnecessary
    C. Conflict is evil
    D. None of the above

10. Restraining forces and structural conflict are best overcome by:

    A. The unfreezing of an old pattern of relationships
    B. The switch to a new pattern through change induced by a change agent
    C. The refreezing of a new pattern of relationships
    D. All of the above
    E. None of the above

NOTES

Chapter 10
CRITICAL THINKING, PLANNING AND PROBLEM SOLVING

LEARNING OBJECTIVES

1. Identify key elements in the definition of a managerial decision.
2. Describe the dynamics involved in the decision-making process.
3. Show the relationship between problem solving and decision-making.
4. Make a distinction between personal and organizational decisions.
5. Discuss what problems may be encountered in decision-making.
6. Identify internal, external, and personal constraints on decision-making.
7. Differentiate between the various types of managerial decisions.
8. Demonstrate steps involved in the rational decision-making process.

QUESTIONS

1. **The criminal intelligence/information cycle describes all but the following:**

   A. Collection
   B. Targeting
   C. Collation
   D. Analysis
   E. Informants

2. **Which of the following is arguably the most important step in decision-making?**

   A. Decision style determination
   B. Selection of solution
   C. Development of possible solutions
   D. Problem identification
   E. Evaluation of decision outcomes

3. **Research indicates that more than _____ % of the repeat calls for service come from _____% addresses in many communities.**

   A. 20% and 40%
   B. 30% and 40%
   C. 50% and 10%
   D. None of the above

4. **Your department is experiencing a series of 20 burglaries in your community. The burglar has a specific modus operandi and his trademark includes urinating in household beds. Your best estimate of his travel distance from his residence in most cases:**

   A. The burglar lives outside the city.
   B. The burglar lives more than 5 miles away.
   C. The burglar lives less than 2 miles away.
   D. None of the above.

5. **Strategic planning is best described as:**

   A. Short term
   B. Long term
   C. Both of the above
   D. None of the above

CHAPTER 11
EVALUATION: HOW WILL WE KNOW WHEN WE HAVE ARRIVED?

LEARNING OBJECTIVES

1. List the reasons why we evaluate.
2. Describe the need for timely evaluations.
3. List the strengths of evaluation research.
4. Define performance indicators.
5. Describe the essential internal and external points of evaluation.
6. List the basic steps in evaluation research.
7. Appraise the need for strategic, tactical and evaluation procedures.

QUESTIONS

1. **The Pareto Principle states that _____ % of the problem in any system results from _____% of the causes.**

   A. 50%-50%
   B. 30%-70%
   C. 80%-20%
   D. None of the above

2. **According to EFFECTIVE POLICE LEADERSHIP, evaluation should include:**

   A. Community policing
   B. Culture and change
   C. Personnel
   D. Integrity and ethics
   E. All of the above

3. "Effectiveness is doing the right things, and efficiency is doing things right." The author of this statement is:

   A. Baker
   B. Hersey
   C. Drucker
   D. None of the above

4. Once the assessment of the present state (Where are we now?) is conducted, the future state (Where are we going?) can be projected. What helps to determine future changes?

   A. Timely evaluations
   B. Assessing strengths
   C. Evaluating staff and information
   D. None of the above

5. The evaluation of community policing primarily concerns:

   A. Fear of crime
   B. Rate of crime
   C. Police performance and effectiveness
   D. All of the above

CHAPTER 12
EFFECTIVE LEADERSHIP:
10 "CAN DO" POINTS

LEARNING OBJECTIVES

1. Describe the need for a community-oriented policing philosophy.
2. Why is character and ethics important in law enforcement?
3. What are the essentials of effective senior leadership?
4. What are the essentials of effective police middle leaders/managers?
5. Why are sergeants and police officers important?
6. Describe what leaders can do to empower officers.
7. Describe how creative and tough training improve police performance.
8. Why is human resources management at the core of police leadership responsibility?
9. Describe the need for effective conflict management.
10. Describe why police officers need to be involved in the planning process.
11. List the reasons why evaluation is necessary to redirect the leadership process.

QUESTIONS

1. According to EFFECTIVE POLICE LEADERSHIP, leadership demands more than trust and character. Leaders must display:

A. Ethics
B. Morality
C. Competence
D. None of the above

2. According to EFFECTIVE POLICE LEADERSHIP, empowering means:

   A. Relinquishing control over the results
   B. Telling the officer how to accomplish the objective
   C. Developing a plan of action for the officer
   D. Evaluate the results for positive outcomes

3. Captains or lieutenants, better known as middle managers/leaders, should:

   A. Not conduct personal inspections
   B. Avoid personal inspections to spare embarrassment
   C. Task others to conduct inspections
   D. Conduct inspections as a primary leadership responsibility

4. When a leader engages in pacing, the:

   A. Leader engages in direct supervision
   B. Leader matches the behavior or gets "in sync"
   C. Leader tells the officer what to do
   D. None of the above

5. In EFFECTIVE POLICE LEADERSHIP, Sergeant Ray Hayes describes:

   A. Democratic leadership
   B. Be, Know and Do Leadership
   C. Participatory management
   D. None of the above

EPILOGUE
FUTURE LEADERSHIP STRATEGIES

LEARNING OBJECTIVES

1. Identify how social change impacts on police operations.
2. List the twelve strategies for future strategic leadership.
3. Define the TQL formula for leadership.
4. Define the COP + POP = COPPS equation.
5. List the order of analysis n the SARA Planning Process.
6. Identify leadership issues concerning GIS crime mapping.
7. List the basic elements of crime analysis.
8. Describe the Compstat leadership process.
9. Define operations and analysis.
10. Describe how leaders can plan for change.

CONCLUSION

> The systematic design for instruction includes four basic progressions:
>
> - ◆ Learning objectives and test bank questions
> - ◆ Case studies and group discussions
> - ◆ Personal assessment paper
> - ◆ Oral board simulated practice experience

- ❖ Each progression builds leadership skills in sequential order.
- ❖ The learning objectives and test bank questions assist in developing basic concepts and content.
- ❖ The learning objectives provide direction for the learner and enhance retention.
- ❖ Moreover, learning objectives reinforce the readings, objective questions and serve as potential essay or oral questions.
- ❖ The case studies and group discussions provide opportunities for application and exchange of ideas and opinions.
- ❖ The personal assessment paper provides the opportunity for critical thinking and the further integration of a personal leadership philosophy.
- ❖ The mock oral board provides a learning simulation that approximates the selection process.
- ❖ This learning opportunity and lead-up activity alleviates anxiety and builds confidence.

NOTES

APPENDIX A
POLICE ADVANCED LEADERSHIP
Seminar Outline

Course Description
Police Leadership Seminar

The Advanced Police Leadership Seminar emphasizes leadership responsibilities at the senior, middle management/leadership and sergeant levels. The seminar focuses on three leadership questions: (1) *Where am I going? How will I get there?* and *How will I know when I have arrived?* The police leadership planning and SARA model ultimately addresses: *Where do I go next?* This seminar explores many of the leadership issues concerning community-oriented and problem-oriented policing.

INSTRUCTOR: _____

TITLE: _____

Table of Contents

Seminar Description	SECTION I
Instructional Methods	SECTION II
Text	SECTION III
Outline and Learning Objectives	SECTION IV
Self-Assessment Assignments	SECTION V
Instructional Procedures	SECTION VI
Assignment Schedule	SECTION VII

INTRODUCTION: AN OVERVIEW

I.   *SEMINAR DESCRIPTION*

This seminar explores many of the issues concerning leadership and problem-oriented policing. The purpose of this course is to enhance the possibility of police leaders developing insight into effective leadership techniques. The seminar serves as a self-assessment leadership process and educational experience.

II.   *INSTRUCTIONAL METHODS*

The advanced officer-training program includes the following professional development assignments:

❖ Learning Objectives	❖ Leadership Assessment
❖ Case Studies	❖ Organizational Analysis Assignment
❖ Objective Test Questions	❖ Practice Promotional Board

III.   *TEXT*

EFFECTIVE POLICE LEADERSHIP: *Moving Beyond Management*, Thomas E. Baker, Looseleaf Law Publications Inc. (800) 647-5547.

IV.   *LEARNING OBJECTIVES AND WRITTEN ASSIGNMENTS – Outlined per Chapter*

Upon successful completion of this seminar, the learner will be able to respond appropriately to each unit of instruction as follows:

Chapter 1
Philosophy: Community-Oriented Policing

  A. Community Oriented Policing
  B. Problem-Oriented Policing
  C. Neighborhood Policing
  D. Leadership Challenge

LEARNING OBJECTIVES

1. Discuss the term "community-oriented policing."
2. Identify community-oriented policing values.
3. Describe how to implement community-oriented policing.
4. Describe some community-oriented policing problems.
5. Define traditional policing.
6. Identify role conflicts that police officers may encounter with the community-oriented policing philosophy.
7. Describe some elements of problem-oriented policing.
8. List the elements of the SARA Planning Process.
9. Describe some basic leadership elements of a Neighborhood Watch Program.

Chapter 2
Police Leadership and Professional Ethics

  A. Assessing The Ethical Climate
  B. Teaching Values And Ethics
  C. Role Modeling The Behaviors
  D. Inspiring Your Officers

LEARNING OBJECTIVES

1. List some elements of the Police Code of Ethics.
2. Describe attributes of an ethical climate.
3. Recite the Law Enforcement Oath of Honor.
4. List the characteristics of ethical police behavior.
5. Conduct a personal assessment of professional and ethical standards.
6. Describe how to build an ethical climate.

7. List the key characteristics of an unethical and ethical climate.
8. Describe the professional ethics model.
9. List four requirements for ethical decision-making.
10. Describe some of the rationalizations that can lead to misconduct on the part of police leaders.

Chapter 3
Police Senior Leadership

A. Developing And Sharing The Vision
B. Charting The Journey
C. Establishing Strategic Objectives
D. Collaboration
E. Delegation

LEARNING OBJECTIVES

1. Discuss the role of the Chief of Police as a strategic leader.
2. Define senior leadership.
3. Identify essential senior leadership responsibilities.
4. Define how senior leaders use indirect leadership to implement their basic leadership functions.
5. Define vision.
6. Describe how to implement vision.
7. Describe the four senior leadership functions.
8. Describe three senior leadership imperatives.
9. Describe the basic elements of social power.

Chapter 4
Middle Management and Leadership

A. Coordinating and Planning
B. Mentoring
C. Coaching
D. Building Teams
E. Empowering and Rewarding

LEARNING OBJECTIVES

1. Describe the self-assessment process.
2. Define the term "middle manager."
3. Define the term "management."
4. Identify the POSDCORB management functions.
5. Differentiate between management and leadership.
6. Describe the role of the manager.
7. List the characteristics of McGregor's Theory X and Theory Y.
8. Differentiate between the following terms: coaching, building teams and empowering.
9. List four management functions.
10. Describe Theory Z.
11. Describe Quality-Circle Programs.

Chapter 5
Sergeants and Police Officers

    A. Sergeants Leading The Way
    B. Leadership By Example
    C. Supervising And Training Teams
    D. Evaluating Performance

LEARNING OBJECTIVES

1. Define leadership.
2. Identify essential sergeant leadership responsibilities.
3. Define the leadership framework.
4. Distinguish between directive and supportive behaviors.
5. Define the four basic leadership styles.
6. Describe the various developmental levels.
7. Apply the appropriate leadership style to the follower's developmental level.
8. Assess the role of the police sergeant in sustaining the ethical climate.
9. Discuss the elements of transforming leadership.

Chapter 6
Motivation and Police Personnel

    A. Defining Excellence
    B. Defining Goals And Objectives
    C. Evaluating Performance
    D. Rewarding Performance

LEARNING OBJECTIVES

1. Define "motivation."
2. Describe the role of senior leaders, middle managers and first line supervisors involving the motivation of police officers.
3. Discuss goal-oriented behavior in the police department.
4. Define the elements of an objective.
5. Describe a work plan.
6. Define Vroom's Theory of Motivation.
7. List methods that may be used to help reverse police cynicism.
8. List the steps in an effective disciplinary process.

Chapter 7
Police Training

    A. Defining The Strategic Training Program
    B. Training That Builds Performance
    C. Training That Builds Morale And Confidence

LEARNING OBJECTIVES

1. Describe the essential outcomes of training.
2. Define strategic training.
3. Identify consequences of inadequate police training.
4. Describe the relationship between training and motivation.
5. Compare senior, middle manager and first line supervisor training responsibilities.
6. Discuss the legal liabilities that may be the consequence of inadequate police training.
7. Identify the steps involved in the development of strategic planning and training.
8. Define active learning.

Chapter 8
Human Resources Management

A. Identifying Strategic Human Resources
B. Character Foundations
C. Excellent Mentorship
D. Coaching Police Officers

LEARNING OBJECTIVES

1. Identify the various strategic objectives necessary for achieving the potential of human resources management.
2. Describe the need for quality police personnel.
3. Identify some of the key federal legislation that ensures the civil rights of an applicant.
4. Define vicarious liability.
5. Define the Management by Objective System.
6. List the basic advantages and disadvantages of an evaluation system.
7. Discuss some of the limitations concerning promotion and advancement in the Twenty-First Century.
8. List the benefits of a police wellness program.
9. Discuss the steps involved in a police suicide prevention program.

Chapter 9
Conflict Management

A. Developing Conflict Management Plans
B. Managing Internal Conflict
C. Managing Community Conflict

LEARNING OBJECTIVES

1. Define conflict.
2. Describe the five stages of conflict.
3. Identify and discuss the most common causes of conflict in police organizations.
4. Describe the differences between functional conflict and dysfunctional conflict.

5. Define intrapersonal and interpersonal conflict.
6. Describe some techniques of conflict management.
7. Discuss some of the strategies for solving interpersonal conflict.
8. Describe how police managers can deal with problem officers.
9. Describe active or focused listening.

Chapter 10
Critical Thinking, Planning and Problem-Solving

    A. **Identifying The Mandates And Present State**
    B. **Describe The Future State**
    C. **Implementing Strategic And Tactical Plans**

LEARNING OBJECTIVES

1. Identify key elements in the definition of a managerial decision.
2. Describe the dynamics involved in the decision-making process.
3. Show the relationship between problem-solving and decision-making.
4. Make a distinction between personal and organizational decisions.
5. Discuss what problems are encountered in decision-making.
6. Identify internal, external, and personal constraints on decision-making.
7. Differentiate between the various types of managerial decisions.
8. Demonstrate steps involved in the rational decision-making process.

Chapter 11
Evaluation: How Will We Know When We Have Arrived?

    A. **Identifying Goals and Objectives**
    B. **Selecting the Evaluation Process**
    C. **Determining Results**
    D. **New Destinations**

LEARNING OBJECTIVES

1. List the reasons why we evaluate.
2. Describe the need for timely evaluations.
3. List the strengths of evaluation.
4. Define performance indicators.
5. Describe the essential internal and external points of evaluation.
6. List the basic steps in evaluation research.
7. Appraise the need for strategic, tactical and evaluation procedures.

Chapter 12
Effective Leadership: 10 "Can Do" Points

    A. Developing A Sense Of Mission
    B. Encouraging Positive Relationships
    C. Encouraging Prudent Risk Taking
    D. Praising The Correct Behaviors

LEARNING OBJECTIVES

1. Describe the need for a community oriented policing philosophy.
2. Why is character and ethics important in law enforcement?
3. What are the essentials of effective senior leadership?
4. What are the essentials of effective police middle leaders/ managers?
5. Why are sergeants and police officers important?
6. Describe what leaders can do to empower officers.
7. Describe how creative and tough training improve police performance.
8. Why is human resources management at the core of police leadership responsibility?
9. Describe the need for effective conflict management.
10. Describe why police officers need to be involved in the planning process.
11. List the reasons why evaluation is necessary to redirect the leadership process.

Epilogue
Future Leadership Strategies

    A. COP and POP
    B. Vision and COPPS
    C. TQL = Excellence
    D. COPPS Planning
    E. Neighborhood Oriented Policing

LEARNING OBJECTIVES

1. Identify how social change impacts on police operations.
2. List the seven strategies for future strategic leadership applications.
3. Define the TQL formula for leadership.
4. Define the COP + POP = COPPS equation.
5. Describe how leaders can plan for change and implement successful strategies.

V. SELF-ASSESSMENT ASSIGNMENT

Assignment 1 – Organizational Analysis

1. Develop and present orally an administrative analysis of a medium-sized (25,000 to 75,000 population city) law enforcement agency including organizational chart, titles of divisions, police titles, territorial divisions, time units, grouping of tasks, levels and lines of authority, specialization, liaison, and functions of each division including the leaders. In addition, add any appraisal and recommendations that will gear the department for changes and future growth.
2. Recite eleven principles of organization for police and public agencies.
3. List and describe the four-step process of authority delegation.
4. Discuss the process of reorganization and the application of organizational principles.
5. Contrast advantages with disadvantages of specialization.
6. Identify the necessity involved in the creation of various enforcement divisions.

Assignment 2 – Leadership Assessment Exercise

1. **PURPOSE:** This written exercise encourages officers to reflect on, formalize and define their personal leadership philosophy. Thinking **"effective leadership"** strategies assists in preparation for police promotion oral boards and enhances your chance for success when you demonstrate confidence!

2. **RECOMMENDATION:** The author recommends rehearsal in simulated situations. Active learning exercises offer a positive learning experience and enhance content retention.

3. **INTRODUCTION:** Your paper should focus on your personal command leadership philosophy. Phrase your comments in "first person" i.e., when "I" become a leader. Compare and contrast what is important to **YOU!**

4. **ORGANIZATIONAL FRAME OF REFERENCE:** Consider a police organization the size of your agency and the rank of police lieutenant or captain. Include important leadership concepts that influence your organization.

5. **ASSESSMENT QUESTIONS:** Your personal assessment should answer the following questions concerning leadership:

   ❖ Where am I going?
   ❖ How will I get there?
   ❖ How will I know when I have arrived?
   ❖ Where do I go next?
   ❖ How do I make my goals understood by others?
   ❖ How can I influence staff and officers?

Include the Following Major Leadership Concepts:

- ❖ Vision
- ❖ Climate
- ❖ Direction
- ❖ Character
- ❖ Values
- ❖ Integrity

SPECIAL NOTE: Refer to the assignment outline for additional information.

VI. INSTRUCTIONAL PROCEDURES

All too often, officers prepare for promotional exams in isolation and fail to make the formal training connections and applications of knowledge. The training seminar, taught with a role-playing and applied laboratory approach, can create opportunities for active learning and application of knowledge gained. The Police Leadership Seminar focuses on management procedures and major leadership issues. The PowerPoint enhanced course includes: case studies, practical learning simulations and practice examinations.

The Case Study Method: Progression 1

The case study method and learning simulations offer opportunities for critical thinking and problem solving applications. Active learning simulations provide opportunities for meaningful group activities that foster critical thinking and leadership applications. This method of leadership training attempts to initiate an active learning approach that applies: (1) critical thinking; (2) problem-solving; (3) decision making; (4) theory and skill applications across the field of law enforcement. The basic pedagogy of active learning emphasizes a cooperative classroom climate in which officers learn from each other.

The case study method has been widely used in the study of law and other academic disciplines. "The case study method, as a classroom pedagogy, has enjoyed a boom in recent years, although it has largely been restricted to courses in education and business, and mostly at the graduate level. Nevertheless, the method is well suited to police training.

The police instructor disseminates twelve or more case studies based on outside research and resources. The officers critique the leadership case studies in small groups of generally three or four officers. Each team presents their solutions on the blackboard, overhead transparencies or PowerPoint. The instructor compares and contrasts the solutions and may make several short comments. Every solution is accepted in a respectful manner.

Leadership Self-Assessment Paper: Progression 2

The paper is a reflective exercise paper, written for self-exploration of one's personal leadership philosophy and leadership style. The exercise explores what the leader stands for, i.e., vision, values and character. The purpose of the paper is three fold, values clarification, and practice for the written and oral board. Refer to the exercise format in this text for further instructions.

Oral Board Practice Sessions: Progression 3

What are some advantages of learning simulations and the related role-playing? The learning simulation enhances performance potential and confidence. Officers learn by playing the role; they internalize the norms and role requirements. Mock promotional boards offered in a formalized setting, provide lead-up activities that reduce anxiety and improve performance. When officers participate as both applicant and board member, they internalize both roles and learn to anticipate questions. More importantly, officers learn to improve their responses.

VII. ASSIGNMENT SCHEDULE FOR INSTRUCTIONAL PROCEDURES

WEEK	READINGS	CHAPTER	DATES
1	Introduction: Strategic Leadership	Introduction	
2	Community Policing and Problem-Oriented Policing	1	
3	Police Values and Ethics	2	
4	Senior Leadership	3	
5	Middle Managers and Leadership	4	
6	Sergeants and Police Officers	5	
7	Motivation of Police Personnel	6	
8	Police Training	7	
9	Human Resources	8	
10	Conflict Management	9	
11	Critical Thinking and Planning	10	
13	Evaluation: How Do We Know We Have Arrived?	11	
14	Effective Leadership: What did We Learn?	12	
15	Epilogue: Future Strategies	Epilogue	

CONCLUSION:

The planning schedule and course outline is flexible. Applications in both training and academic environments offer a variety of options. The instructor may condense the schedule for regional training programs. The foundation for training and academic excellence remains **organization** and **preparation**.

APPENDIX B
PERSONAL ASSESSMENT EXERCISE

1. **PURPOSE:** This written exercise encourages officers to reflect on, formalize and define their personal leadership philosophy. Thinking **"effective leadership"** strategies assists in preparation for police promotion oral boards and enhances your chance for success when you demonstrate confidence!

2. **RECOMMENDATION:** This exercise is important for every leader because if the leader does not know where they are going, how can they expect officers to follow? Refer to *EFFECTIVE POLICE LEADERSHIP: MOVING BEYOND MANAGEMENT* when you formulate your personal assessment.

3. **INTRODUCTION:** Your paper should focus on your personal command leadership philosophy. Phrase your comments in "first person" i.e., when "I" become a leader. Compare and contrast what is important to **YOU!**

4. **ORGANIZATIONAL FRAME OF REFERENCE:** Consider a police organization the size of your agency and the rank of police lieutenant or captain. Include important leadership concepts that influence your organization.

5. **GENERAL INSTRUCTIONS:** Your personal assessment should answer the following questions concerning leadership:

- ❖ Where am I going?
- ❖ How will I get there?
- ❖ How will I know when I have arrived?
- ❖ Where do I go next?
- ❖ How do I make my goals understood by others?
- ❖ How can I influence staff and officers?

Include the Following
Major Leadership Concepts:

- ❖ Vision
- ❖ Climate
- ❖ Direction
- ❖ Character
- ❖ Values
- ❖ Integrity

Leadership Exercise Outline

PARAGRAPH #1 (INTRODUCTION)	COMPARE AND CONTRAST
Controlling Idea ❖ Topic sentence ❖ How can you influence the organization? ❖ Where am I going? ❖ How will I get there? ❖ How will I know when I have arrived? ❖ Vision ❖ Direction ❖ Climate	**Personal Philosophy and Concepts:** ❖ First person "I" i.e., when I become a middle manager/leader of my police agency ❖ Vision (use your own terminology i.e., focus or purpose) ❖ Direction – How do you motivate? ❖ Begin with an interesting quotation/story that motivates the reader to continue reading
PARAGRAPH #2 (TRANSITION)	COMPARE AND CONTRAST
Leadership Direction: ❖ Identify department mandates ❖ How can you make your goals understood by your officers? ❖ Direct/indirect leadership ❖ Character and values ❖ Ethical accountability ❖ Mission statement ❖ Vision	**Your Terminology and Concepts:** ❖ How will you develop key relationships and officer trust? ❖ How can you influence your department and officers? ❖ Identify officers' personal goals and objectives ❖ Teach and mentor officers

PARAGRAPH #3	COMPARE AND CONTRAST
Leadership Theory:	**Building the Ethical Climate**
❖ Principles of leadership	❖ Assess the ethical climate
❖ Inspiring officers	❖ Teach values and ethics
❖ Professional ethics	❖ Respect officers
❖ Role modeling	❖ Being the standard bearer

PARAGRAPH #4	COMPARE AND CONTRAST
Middle Managers/Leaders in Action:	**Your Personal Philosophy and Opinion:**
❖ Establishing purpose	❖ What are you trying to accomplish?
❖ Establishing motivation	❖ How will you develop support?
❖ Your concept of an effective organization	❖ How will you communicate and manage conflict?
❖ The balance between direct and indirect leadership	❖ How do you know when you are being effective?
❖ The appropriate leadership style to use with officers	❖ How will you influence when you cannot be there personally?
❖ How will you modify your approach to decision making?	❖ How will you get your officers to buy into your concept of the operation?
❖ Strategic training	

PARAGRAPH #5	COMPARE AND CONTRAST
Unit Leadership and Development	**Your Personal Philosophy and Opinion:**
❖ Diagnostic skills	❖ Where are your followers going?
❖ Diagnosing competence and commitment	❖ Evaluation of vision, mission and value statements
❖ Prescribing the most effective leader behaviors	❖ How will you evaluate completed goals and objectives?
❖ Command climate	❖ Working with staff - assessing weaknesses and strengths
❖ Evaluation of community policing, culture and change, personnel, integrity and ethics, community and evaluation strategies	❖ Building teams
	❖ Empowering and rewarding officers

PARAGRAPH #6	COMPARE AND CONTRAST
Conclusion: Brief Summary ❖ Charting the course ❖ Evaluation of vision goals and objectives ❖ Where do we go now? ❖ Desired future state	**Concluding Remarks:** ❖ Reaffirm important observations ❖ Restatement of controlling idea ❖ Concluding statement that enhances and supports your personal leadership assessment

Errata Sheet: Chapter 4, Answers to Questions 8 & 9

APPENDIX C: ANSWER KEY FOR OBJECTIVE QUESTIONS

1	2	3	4	5	6	7	8	9	10	11	12
1.B	1.C	1.C	1.B	1.B	1.B	1.B	1.C	1.D	1.E	1.C	1.C
2.C	2.D	2.B	2.C	2.D	2.D	2.E	2.C	2.D	2.D	2.E	2.D
3.B	3.B	3.C	3.C	3.A	3.B	3.C	3.D	3.C	3.C	3.C	3.D
4.A	4.C	4.A	4.D	4.D	4.D	4.A	4.B	4.B	4.C	4.A	4.B
5.D	5.E	5.C	5.E	5.C	5.D	5.C	5.A	5.B	5.B	5.D	5.B
		6.A	6.C	6.C				6.B			
		7.C	7.B	7.D				7.C			
		8.C	8.E	8.D				8.B			
		9.B	9.4.	9.B				9.A			
		10.C		10.B				10.D			
				11.C							
				12.A							
				13.D							
				14.A							
				15.C							
				16.D							
				17.A							
				18.B							
				19.D							
				20.D							

APPENDIX C: ANSWER KEY FOR OBJECTIVE QUESTIONS

1	2	3	4	5	6	7	8	9	10	11	12
1. B	1. C	1. C	1. B	1. B	1. B	1. B	1. C	1. D	1. E	1. C	1. C
2. C	2. D	2. B	2. C	2. D	2. D	2. E	2. C	2. D	2. D	2. E	2. D
3. B	3. B	3. C	3. C	3. A	3. B	3. C	3. D	3. C	3. C	3. C	3. D
4. A	4. C	4. A	4. D	4. D	4. D	4. A	4. B	4. B	4. C	4. A	4. B
5. D	5. E	5. C	5. E	5. C	5. D	5. C	5. A	5. B	5. B	5. D	5. B
		6. A	6. C	6. C				6. B			
		7. C	7. B	7. D				7. C			
		8. C	8. B	8. D				8. B			
		9. B	9. E	9. B				9. A			
		10. C	10. D	10. B				10. D			
				11. C							
				12. A							
				13. D							
				14. A							
				15. C							
				16. D							
				17. A							
				18. B							
				19. D							
				20. D							

NOTES

NOTES

NOTES

OTHER TITLES OF INTEREST
FROM LOOSELEAF LAW PUBLICATIONS, INC.

Effective Police Leadership 2ⁿᵈ Edition
Moving Beyond Management
by Thomas E. Baker, Lt. Col. MP USAR (Ret.)

Police Management Examinations
by Larry Jetmore

Police Sergeant Examination Preparation Guide
by Larry Jetmore

Police Supervisor's Test Manual
by Cliff Mariani

Police Promotion Manual
by William J. McCullough

How to be Successful on *"Written"* Assessment Exercises for Police Promotion
by Donald J. Schroeder & Frank A. Lombardo

How to be Successful on *"Oral"* Assessment Exercises for Police Promotion
by Donald J. Schroeder & Frank A. Lombardo

Terrorism Prevention and Response - 2ⁿᵈ Edition
The Definitive Law Enforcement Guide to Prepare for Terrorist Activity
by Cliff Mariani

Use of Force
Expert Guidance for Decisive Force Response
by Brian A. Kinnaird

Advanced Vehicle Stop Tactics
Skills for Today's Survival Conscious Officer
by Michael T. Rayburn

62

Advanced Patrol Tactics
Skills for Today's Street Cop
by Michael T. Rayburn

Handgun Combatives
by Dave Spaulding

Defensive Living - 2ⁿᵈ Edition
Preserving Your Personal Safety Through Awareness, Attitude and Armed Action
by Ed Lovette & Dave Spaulding

Deadly Force
Constitutional Standards, Federal Policy Guidelines, and Officer Survival
by John Michael Callahan, Jr.

Path of the Warrior - 2ⁿᵈ Edition
An Ethical Guide to Personal & Professional Development in the Field of Criminal Justice
by Larry F. Jetmore

The COMPSTAT Paradigm
Management Accountability in Policing, Business and the Public Sector
by Vincent E. Henry, CPP, Ph.D.

How to Really, *Really* Write Those Boring Police Reports
by Kimberly Clark

The New Age of Police Supervision and Management
A Behavioral Concept
by Michael A. Petrillo & Daniel R. DelBagno

(800) 647-5547   **www.LooseleafLaw.com**